Precision Targeting

B. Vincent

Published by RWG Publishing, 2021.

PRECISION TARGETING

First edition. June 10, 2021.

Written by B. Vincent.

Also by B. Vincent

Affiliate Marketing
Affiliate Marketing

Standalone
Affiliate Recruiting
Business Layoffs & Firings
Business and Entrepreneur Guide
Business Remote Workforce
Career Transition
Project Management
Precision Targeting

Table of Contents

Precision Targeting

Hello, and welcome to this course on **Precision Ad Targeting**, in this course, we're going to cover how to really hone in on the exact prospects you're looking for. This course is divided into three modules. *Module 1* gives you a brief intro to precision targeting concepts, *Module 2* goes over geo-targeting and *Module 3* covers demographics, interests, and placements. By the time this course is over, you'll know how to target your audience with incredible precision, so without further ado, let's dive into the first module. Okay guys, welcome to Module 1, in this module, our expert will give you a brief intro to precision targeting concepts, so get ready to take some notes and let's jump right in.

Module 1

All right, so in this book, we're going to do a quick academic overview, and then we'll jump into the actual over-the-shoulder stuff in the next module. So basically the type of precision targeting we're going over today, refers to using a combination of multiple layers, if you will, of targeting parameters all used on top of each other to produce what we might call a hyper- targeted audience. Now these multiple layers consist of geographic targeting, demographic targeting, interest targeting, placement targeting, and sometimes intent targeting, and we'll talk about that a little bit later.

The power of precision targeting comes from the overlapping of these layers. Now real, super precision targeting would theoretically include a minimum of three of those layers, preferably four, if it's applicable. And it's important to note that within those parameter categories, you can also have multiple overlapping layers inside of them. So, within geographic targeting or within interests targeting, you can have some overlap within those, and you'll see what I mean shortly. Let me give you an example, and this is kind of an outside the box example. Let's say we're targeting Indian or South Asian business owners in the US on Facebook. So, we're going to have ad images geared towards that demographic and the people in the background images of our landing pages will have that demographic or ethnic background in mind when we create them, and so on. Here is how we might organize our layers. First off there's geographic, so let's say we did some research and found out which metropolitan areas in the US had the highest Indian or South Asian populations. We would then use that information to target only those geographic areas in our Facebook ad campaign, and then on top of that, we add a demographic layer. Let's say we estimate, or we do some research that most of these business owners are probably in their forties or older, so we set that age as another demographic layer on top of our geographic layer. Now you cannot target by ethnicity on Facebook for obvious reasons, but if you think outside the box a little bit, you can find ways to achieve the same purpose indirectly.

There are some demographics and behavioral options that you can use and browse through, including X Patriots. You can choose ex-pats, people who previously lived in India or another South Asian country, or you could choose people designated as having family members who live abroad. Since that's often the case with these demographic categories, since they're often just first, second or third generation immigrant families, then they've often got extended families in their countries of origin, who they still remain in close contact with, so they might pop up under that category. By itself, that doesn't sound like much, but when you overlap these parameters together, you're actually tightening that targeting circle more and more around exactly who we're looking to target. And as you saw there, that was an example of layers within layers for the demographic's category.

Now let's talk about interest targeting and this is amazing because it becomes almost magical if you think outside the box.

Remember we can't target based on ethnicity, but let me ask you this, who likes Bollywood movies? I mean sure, Bollywood has a significant international fan base, it's awesome, but on the whole, what group of people do you think make up the majority of Bollywood fans in the USA? Yes, probably Americans of South Asian descent or Indian descent. So, when you choose the Facebook interest Bollywood movies as an interest, along with other Bollywood related interests. Like let's say Bollywood network or a common Bollywood TV channel, those are all there on Facebook to choose from. If you choose those, you're getting into hyper-targeting, but let's add another layer now. This time we would narrow the audience by using **And** logic instead of **Or** logic, meaning we want to make sure that this next layer has to be held in addition to the one that we just specified rather than **Or**. So, we don't want someone who likes Bollywood or is also a business owner because that'll completely ruin the entire targeting process. We want someone who likes Bollywood and is a business owner. And by the way, depending on what platform you're using, like for example Facebook, Facebook categorizes its business owner targeting metrics as interests sometimes. Some of them are job titles, there's a whole bunch of different categories inside of Facebook, so when you're doing that search for business owner related terms inside of your Facebook targeting, you'll see that pop up, and that's just the way Facebook arbitrarily categorizes things. But the important thing here again is that it is **and** logic, so we're narrowing it down, we want people who are Bollywood fans and are business owners.

Let's review this whole targeting concept that we've set up. Our ads will only be shown to people who are in areas with large South Asian populations and who are in their forties and who have extended family overseas and who are interested in Bollywood and our small business owners. You see what just happened? We just precision targeted the exact group that we wanted to display our ads to. And if you make your ad creatives match this group, for example, using images of people who fit this demographic, well then, you're going to have a ton of success with your ad campaigns. Now we didn't touch on website placements here, since this is just for everyone on Facebook, we didn't touch on intent targeting, which generally means search targeting because again, this is just for everybody on Facebook. But we used three of our targeting layers and also some layers within layers and it produced a highly targeted audience for us. So hopefully that gives you an idea of the kind of precision targeting that you can do with your ads, again, it's all about thinking outside the box. In the next module, we're going to actually jump into the over-the- shoulder mode and do some hands-on training and some geo-targeting.

Module 2

Welcome to Module 2, in this module, our expert will go over geo-targeting, so get ready to take some notes and let's jump right in.

All right let's go over some of the ways that we can use geo-targeting in our advertising and keep in mind, this is just one layer of targeting that you should plan on overlapping with other layers like we discussed in the first module. Now geo-targeting doesn't just mean picking a specific city or region, although that's obviously something that you're going to do if you're a brick and mortar or a local business. Instead, geo-targeting means choosing locations based on your existing market research and choosing an area that has the greatest number of people who you're trying to attract and convert. So, before we do any geographic targeting, we first need to do some geographic research and we'll use a couple of examples here. First off, let's say that we're selling something specifically to affluent people. Let's say it's a real estate related offer or arts and antiquities, an investment opportunity, or even a special new golf club that we're trying to sell since the golf niche tends to skew a little bit towards the affluent side. Well, one of the coolest tricks for that kind of research is the US Census Bureau at census.gov. In this case, we're going to use the median household income map that they have over there on their website, and we're going to try and target a particularly rich part of the United States.

So, let's have a look here, it looks like the green that we're seeing indicates a median household income of 65,000 or higher, which is pretty darn high. From what I understand, just looking at this map, but also from what I've heard, the east coast around Virginia and Maryland are probably the richest parts of the US. Or not necessarily the richest, but the areas where there are counties with the highest median household income and that may or may not be correct. That's just what I've heard, and so we're just going to use that as a little clue, a little lead for an area to start our research just for this example. Let's have a look here and zoom into Virginia, and we're looking at 78,000 median household income, 80,000 right there in Clark County, $142,000 median household income in Loudon County. We've got 116, 124, so this whole area here seems absolutely ripe for exactly what we're looking for, so let's go ahead and focus on Loudon County right here. I'm not sure if I'm pronouncing that correctly or not. And let's do a geographic targeting net that we're going to cast just over this county here, and we're going to do this inside of Google ads. So we'll come over here to our Google ad campaign, let's come down here to the location section, enter another location, and what we could do is go to advanced search and narrow in via the map. Let's go ahead and zoom in that area of Virginia, we were looking at.

You could put a manually created radius, you could drop a pin here and say hey, I want everything within 20 miles or 30 miles. Since we actually know the name of the county though, let's try typing it in and see, yeah, there you go, pre-fills. So, let's go with target Loudon County right there, and look, it's right next to the capital, Washington DC. So maybe that's part of why it's such an affluent county as far as its median household income. But there you have it, we've just selected that county, and only people within that county are going to see our ads, so that fits our desire to target rich people. So, we would hit save and that targeting would be saved into our ad campaign, and that's one layer. Once again, that's not everything, that sounds really cool, and it might make you want to jump and start running an ad like this, but that's just one layer. For precision targeting, we want to combine this layer with other layers, which we'll do in the next module. But first before we leave this one, let's toy around with another example.

So that was Google ads, let's try geo-targeting with Facebook ads, and instead of doing the rich people targeting example this time, let's say we're selling a product designed to help people quit smoking. What we want is some smoking research, some smoking geographics and demographics, and a great way to do that is once again, we're going to be relying on a .gov here. In this case, it's cdc.gov, CDC has a whole bunch of data on people who use cigarettes, here's adult cigarette use throughout the United States, and it doesn't do it by county. I bet if we dug really hard, we could find things based on counties and cities. We won't do that for this example, almighty Google is your friend there though, but it looks like the heaviest smoking counties here are going to be in the South and the Midwest area. The darkest ones here looks like around a quarter of people in West Virginia, Kentucky, and Arkansas smoke and close to that same number in these surrounding areas, but that's cigarette use. A lot of people don't want to quit smoking though, and if our product is geared towards people who want to quit. Look at this Quitline is a service where all the data and stats are tracked by the CDC, and this is one of those call-in services where people actually get assistance with quitting smoking. What we can do here is we could look at the number of incoming calls per 10,000 people in the state, and look at that. First off, what we know is that the smokers in West Virginia, Kentucky, and Arkansas apparently don't want to quit too bad according to this data. But it looks like our hottest spots would be South Dakota and Oklahoma because we have 39, almost 40 and almost 38 people per 10,000 population who are calling in asking for help with quitting smoking. So that would be a perfect opportunity to sell a quit smoking related product.

In our case here, and this is where research comes in handy, I happen to know that South Dakota's population, the entire state is less than a million, it's around 800,000 or so, whereas Oklahoma is around 4 million. Even though it's slightly less, per 10,000 here in Oklahoma versus South Dakota, that overall group is actually much larger, it's actually over four times as large versus South Dakota. And so, I'm going to go with Oklahoma here and let's go ahead and go into our Facebook ads and do some geographic targeting for these people who want to quit smoking in Oklahoma. So, let's come on over here to our Facebook ad campaign, we're going to come over here to locations, and let's just select the entire state of Oklahoma. And what we're looking at there is 2,900,000 people. Now remember of that, roughly 40 per 10,000 have called Quitline for help quitting. Now your average person who's trying to quit smoking probably does not call Quitline. That does not mean that it's just 40, per 10,000 people who are trying to quit, what that means is that's a significant indicator, a signal, that a very large number of people, at least comparative, when you compare it to the rest of the United States are trying to quit beyond that 40 per 10,000. And this is actually a pretty good area.

Now, the quit smoking market is probably not the biggest market in the world because most people these days have already quit smoking and are not smoking. We live in kind of a post smoking culture or era. But as far as the smoking or the quit smoking market goes, this is actually a pretty sweet place to target. If we really wanted to, let's say we did some more digging into the county or the city level statistics, assuming that that's out there, that we could search and try to just target Tulsa, Oklahoma City, or a specific area inside of Oklahoma. But for our purposes right now, for our little quit smoking scenario, this is actually a pretty good shot group for us to target with a quit smoking ad, and it's as simple as that. You know, you go, you find good sources, reliable sources for data to do your market research, and then you target accordingly, just like we did for the affluent folks in the Google ads example. And that's the same thing here in the Facebook example with the people who are trying to quit smoking. The big thing to remember though, is we're not here just to geo-target, that was just the purpose of this module. The purpose of the overall course is precision targeting, which means combining this geographic layer with other layers of targeting. So, what we would want to dig down further into with the quit smoking crowd would be their interests on Facebook that indicate someone is trying to quit smoking? Are there popular quit smoking books or programs that might pop up in the interest, and we can grab people who are associated with that. Are there age ranges, does the data show that there are age ranges or gender differences? As far as which demographic group is more likely to be attempting to quit smoking and so on and so forth. So, there's a whole bunch of things we can do here. This is just the geographic targeting aspect of it, and its super-duper useful when combined with everything else. So in the next module, we're going to be looking at specifically the remaining layers of demographic, interest and placement targeting and how we can overlap all of those together to really hone in on the perfect prospect that we're trying to get our ads in front of.

Module 3

All right, welcome to Module 3, in this module, our expert will go over demographics, interests, and placements. So, get ready to take some notes and let's jump right in.

All right, so this where we tie everything together. We're going to do a full stack of multiple overlapping of targeting to really precisely zoom in on the exact prospect that we're trying to track down. Of the scenarios and theoretical examples that we used; we're going to be focusing on two this time. So, within Facebook ads, we're going to be focusing on that example where we were trying to target Indian or South Asian American business owners. For the Google ads example, we're going to be using the scenario where we were trying to target people who are affluent in that special rich part of Virginia. And let's say we're trying to sell them a golf club, so for starters here inside of Facebook, let's look at our targeting. I know we theorized that we might've done some research and figured out where the highest population in the US was of Indian or South Asian immigrants or people of Indian or South Asian descent. We're going to pretend that we didn't okay or we'll pretend that we did, but we're not actually going to mess with that, here we're going to mess with the other demographics that we chose. For example, we said 40 plus was what we were looking for in that example, and so we're going to go with the 40 here. For this one, let's say 65

13

plus, that gives us people over the age of 40. We'll say that gender was not a factor, and for demographics, let's go ahead and go into the detailed targeting and demographics and let's browse and see if we can find that ex-pat example that we're talking about.

So here's ex-pats, we could choose people who lived at one point in India, which is right here, and that would actually give us a pretty small group of people, so I'm not sure if I like that. And it's not that this represents a demographic reality, this only includes those people who have done things online that identify by themselves to Facebook and its data collection processes as having formerly lived in India. Which is probably a minority of people who actually have formerly lived in India. Although it's really cool and you might use this sometimes, we're going to sidestep this one. We're going to focus more on using our interest targeting like Bollywood to do what I think is a job of targeting people who are from South Asia and living in the United States, or who are descended from those who were originally from South Asia. Now we could do family of those who live abroad. I think that would give us a pretty big, shocked group, that's 3.8 million there, and that's versus 110 million. So, we could do that, let's leave that unselected here though, and let's go with the other things we were talking about first. Let's say Bollywood movies, so we've got 4.6 million people who are interested in Bollywood movies.

Let's see if there are any other Bollywood-related interests. Music of Bollywood, okay, but as you can see that kind of overlaps, it's the same group of 4.6 million. Let's try again. We see Bollywood, these two here are probably pretty sizable, that's actually a Bollywood network or channel if I'm guessing correctly. So, Bollywood, NBC, Bollywood again, as you can see that potential reach is not getting bigger than 4.6 million, nothing has changed here. Let's see, Bollywood now, Bollywood diaries, Bollywood express, Bollywood tabloid, actress, actresses, times. So, the biggest one I saw here was the Bollywood now and still that potential reach has not grown at all, which means these all overlap with each other. By the way, this is all **and** logic, which means anybody who likes this one, but doesn't like this one, again, based on Facebook's collection of people's behaviors and such online. And now that we've got Bollywood selected, let's just for grins, let's go to browse and let's choose that behavior, let's go the ex-pats and family of those who live abroad and see what happens to that number group; I'm just curious. Okay, so with the **and** logic, it's 8.1 million now. Now let's remove it, and let's say that we're going to narrow our audience and go to behaviors this time, and you go to ex-pats and families of those who live abroad. Let's see what happens. Yeah, that's just too tight, it's just too tight. So again, it's one of those situations where it's really cool, you could envision yourself using it if you needed to, but I'm pretty confident that this is a better audience right here, the one that happens to be interested in Bollywood.

So here we're going with our 'and also must match' meaning the **and** logic here inside of this field; make sure you're using this one. Let's go ahead and do business owner. All right, so let's see here, employers, business owner, business owner an interest, business owner as a job title, small business owner as an employer, business owner/engineer. And while we're going through these, we're looking at that size, audience size in the little window to the right. All right, so the biggest one for business owner is this one here at 23 million, and that brings us down pretty small. Let's expand that by getting as much business owner related stuff as we can into this portion of our **and** logic. So, let's go with business owner/engineer, I got 237, the small business owner, that's probably a magazine I assume, okay potential reach is still the same. Independent business owner, these are all pretty small numbers. Business ownership, small business owners, plural, and that's a behavior inside of Facebook, so Facebook has seen a behavior of some sort with its data collection that says these people actually are business owners, as opposed to the interest, which is 8.1 million. Let's go with the behavior here and see what happens, nice, so our audience almost doubled there. Well it went from two eight, zero to four, three, zero. Let's see if we can get a little bit bigger. Small business administration, so people interested in the SBA are probably business owners, more often than not, so that brings us up to almost 600,000. Let's see, small business Saturday, small business owners here in interests, and it's 8.1 million, let's try that. Okay, we're at 620,000, so getting bigger. I don't want to touch the small business Saturday, that's really cool, but a lot of consumers are interested in small business Saturday because it's about consumers helping small businesses, so I'm going to skip that one. Small business software, a lot of this is just intuition and intuition tells me that people who are interested in small business software would definitely be people who actually have businesses or the vast majority of them at least. Let's try operator, owner operator, that's a good one, 640 now, let's see if we can come up with anything else. Maybe restaurant owner, that's pretty small, 32,000.

So, you can keep drilling down, the important thing here though is that we've got **and** logic combining people who seem to be interested in business ownership or have a past indicator of business ownership in the opinion of Facebook's data collection, combined with people who fit that and like Bollywood. Which tells me that this number right here, 640,000, I'm pretty confident that we have a lot of business owners of Indian or South Asian descent within that number. So, when you combine that with the other things, we mentioned such as the location targeting, if you were to have done that research and the age, this really is going to be a powerful way to target that group. And again, it gets around the issue of not being able to targets an ethnicity or a specific type of descent directly on Facebook, which again, for obvious reasons, I have that disabled, they have that as not even an option. For some reason you needed to run this type, and I know it sounds goofy, why are you choosing to track down specifically people from one part of the world. It's because it's the perfect example of how powerful precision targeting can be when you overlap all of this stuff together. I don't know that there's any practical reason to do this type of targeting scenario that we used for this example, this just shows you the extreme of how zoomed in and really honed in you can be on the perfect prospect.

So, let's move over to a Google ads example now, and like I said, we'll be using the affluent targeting that we had done in the previous module where we're trying to find people who are really rich in that county in Virginia, and that is right over here. So, we've got our Loudon County, Virginia location targeted here. Let's go down to audiences. Now in audiences, you can do some pretty cool things, it's kind of like Facebook, where they gather indicators of interest and then behavior and so on and so forth. So, we go after people who are interested in banking and finance would probably be more affluent people. We could go after people who definitely own their home, I would say that's almost certain that we would want to target those people there. We could go after some demographic indicators, such as the top 10% of household income, so we would remove all of this and just go after the top 10% here; that's one thing that we could do. We could go after website placements, now this is a big one, and we actually have data on this. Thanks to Google Analytics, we've got a lot of information on the most visited websites, somewhere on here, here we go. The websites that are most visited by the largest percentage, the upper 10% of household income, basically. So, 150,000 plus household income, the Real Deal is a website, it's a real estate website, 27.2% of their visitors have that or higher household income. That's pretty cool, that's pretty useful to know a crunch-base of finance site. DC Urban Mom, lifestyle parenting 23.8 or $150,000 or more. We would skip that one, keeping in mind, we want everything to be relevant and if we're going after golf clubs, if that's what we're selling, that is a hobby that tends to skew towards males, and so we would probably skip the Urban Mom one here, for traders finance, because that's 23.4.

So let me show you, let's say we were going to go through this, we're going to grab the underlined realdeal.com and underlined crunchbase.com, we could literally make our ads up here specifically on that. Let's say the real deal.com, let's see if anything comes up here, the real deal.com, boom, so now we've selected that as a placement, we could go to crunchbase.com. I want to think about that for a second. Website called crunchbase.com, now it's theoretically possible that that's not targetable for some reason, let's come over here and look and make sure I had that crunchbase.com, is finance. So crunchbase.com looks like it's not directly targetable, so we would have to skip that one. Let's see, DC Urban Mom talked about that already, let's say MarketWatch, that one sounds familiar, one- fifth of all of their visitors have a household income of 150,000 or more, so let's do marketwatch.com. I've spent some time on MarketWatch, and I know that there are Google ad banner placements all over their website, sidebar up at the top, the banner area, marketwatch.com. For some reason, it's not letting me choose that specific one though, that's interesting. Now it does let me target their YouTube channel, so that's cool, ad lets me target their mobile apps and that's cool. But the website seems to have some type of a setting, I'm assuming that prevents people from specifically singling them out for a website targeting for ad placements, and that was also the case with Crunchbase, if you'll recall.

So, let's see if we can keep searching and find another one, let's say open table is a lifestyle food site, there's Leonardo DiCaprio right there, and right there is MarketWatch. I've got my ad-block enabled right now, so we can't see, but usually you would see banner ads here, ads in the sidebar and they're all Google display network ads. Let's try opentable.com, boom, so we could add that, and basically if you just start piling up based on data available, all of these different websites and placements, and the website traffic is an indicator of their audience in general. You could do what we did with MarketWatch and also target their YouTube channels and so on and so forth, and their apps, if they have mobile apps, you can run ads on there. Wherever the placements exist and wherever you can get them to cross and correspond with where the data says that your audience is. In this case, it seems like a lot of affluent people hang out on these websites and frequent these brands, that's going to help out quite a bit. And that's about as laser targeted as you can get, saying I want it to show up on these specific websites, apps, or YouTube channels and that's pretty powerful. So, we basically targeted in this example, the richest county in Virginia, possibly in the United States, but certainly in Virginia at least. And we've got the top 10 and the top 20% of household income demographics selected, and we've got a whole bunch of websites, apps, and some YouTube channels, specifically targeted ads places that rich people are known to frequent quite a bit. And that's pretty powerful. We've got a whole bunch of overlapping of targeting, that's a precisely targeted ad.

Now I want to mention one thing, we don't have to actually do it because it's really simple, you've seen it a thousand times, it's search advertising. At the very beginning in Module 1, we talked about how you can actually combine another layer called intent and intent basically just means people who are currently looking for something, they currently want something. So, a person who is literally right there on Google or Bing typing in, *I want to buy a golf club*, or *where to buy golf clubs,* that person at that moment intends to buy a golf club, and that's incredibly powerful, that's huge. And so if you can combine some of these, like the geographic location and the income level with search ads on Google, instead of like this one, for example, is a display ad, this what we're doing for this particular scenario. But if we were to do a search ad and it would show just the people who are searching for golf club related keywords, meaning they intend to buy one, that's why they're on their laptop right now is to buy one. I mean, there's nothing more powerful than that and combine it with income level and their geographic location, that's about as precision targeted as you can get. And that is incredibly powerful to be able to reach out to people when they're looking for something. So, Google search ads combined with this other information here would also be super-duper powerful, but that pretty much sums it up guys.

We saw how to layer all of these different targeting parameters together on Facebook, how to layer them together here inside of Google. We talked about all the different layers of targeting that you can have, we did a couple of different scenarios, and perhaps one of the most important ones here is the research aspect. Depending on what country you're targeting, a lot of this stuff is going to be public information, formal, official public information. There's also plenty of private institutions and entities that do this kind of stuff. Gallup for example is a polling company, Pew research, there are so many different entities that do private research, private polling and data collection that can also be super-duper useful to you. In many cases for those, you're going to have to pay sometimes for a membership to access some of their data, but a lot of their stuff has also been published publicly in journals and in the news.

So ultimately, Google is your friend, anywhere that you can find demographic data that's going to help you target people and figure out how and where to track them down. And if you can include the gift of thinking outside the box like we did with the Bollywood thing, you can really open up some incredible doors, as far as getting straight to just a direct line directly to your perfect exact prospect that you're trying to track down. So hopefully this was useful information for you guys, and you can go out there and put this to use in your next ad campaign.

Don't miss out!

Visit the website below and you can sign up to receive emails whenever B. Vincent publishes a new book. There's no charge and no obligation.

https://books2read.com/r/B-A-QWUO-TJLPB

BOOKS 2 READ

Connecting independent readers to independent writers.

Also by B. Vincent

Affiliate Marketing
Affiliate Marketing

Standalone
Affiliate Recruiting
Business Layoffs & Firings
Business and Entrepreneur Guide
Business Remote Workforce
Career Transition
Project Management
Precision Targeting

About the Publisher

Accepting manuscripts in the most categories. We love to help people get their words available to the world.

Revival Waves of Glory focus is to provide more options to be published. We do traditional paperbacks, hardcovers, audio books and ebooks all over the world. A traditional royalty-based publisher that offers self-publishing options, Revival Waves provides a very author friendly and transparent publishing process, with President Bill Vincent involved in the full process of your book. Send us your manuscript and we will contact you as soon as possible.

Contact: Bill Vincent at rwgpublishing@yahoo.com www.rwgpublishing.com